# Why I Hate Republicans:
## A Guide for Moderates

© Will MacPheat

I originally began with the byline, "*A Guide for Liberals*." Then I realized that we liberals already have it figured out.

Also, some time ago, I realized that Republicans fall into two categories: (1) rich people who realize that it *is* in their economic interest to be Republicans and (2) poor people who are too ignorant or too stupid to realize that it is *not* in their best interests to be Republican. So there is no point in aiming at either group. Moderates, then, seemed the only group that might be persuaded.

My reasons for disliking and distrusting Republicans appear on the following pages.

Why I Hate Republicans…

1.  John Boehner looks mean.

Why I Hate Republicans…


2. Ann Coulter.

Why I Hate Republicans…


3.  Rush Limbaugh.

Why I Hate Republicans…

4. "Trickle Down" Economics.

The first President Bush called this "voodoo economics" and rightfully so.

There is an obvious flaw in the Trickle Down theory that, for some reason, no one seems to have figured out in thirty years. If the greatest mass of consumers (the middle and lower classes) don't have the money to buy things, or don't feel secure enough to buy them, no amount of tax cuts to the rich will stimulate the economy.

When people are not buying from a business, its rich owner will not hire more workers. There would be no increase in income to justify the hiring of additional workers.

Why I Hate Republicans…


5. A trickle is a flow of water so tiny that one would have difficulty drinking from it. Why on earth would anyone vote for THAT? Let alone make it the basis for an economic policy.

Why I Hate Republicans…


6. My boss is a Republican.

Why I Hate Republicans…


7. Republicans focus too much on the "me" side of issues and not the good of the country, all the while waving their flags and proclaiming their patriotism.

This is why the great social programs are passed by Democrats – the programs that are for the good of the country and make us better as a society, not richer as individuals.

When I was canvassing for an environmental cause recently, I was often asked, "Is this a tax?" If I answered, "no," people would argue with me. Finally, I realized that the better response was to say, "You know, the patriotic question is, 'What does this do for our country?'"

Why I Hate Republicans…


8. Bush II, who should be tried as a traitor.

Why I Hate Republicans…

9. If you have to call something "The Patriot Act," you should probably conclude that it is just the opposite.

Why I Hate Republicans…

10. Waving the flag and yelling, "We're the best," doesn't simply make it so.

Why I Hate Republicans…

11. Justice Scalia, in a recent dissent wrote, "This Court has *never* held that the Constitution forbids the execution of a convicted defendant who has had a full and fair trial but is later able to convince a *habeas* court that he is 'actually' innocent." Justice Scalia was joined in this dissent by Justice Thomas.

Justice Scalia was appointed by Ronald Reagan, a Republican. Justice Thomas was appointed by Bush I, also a Republican.

I have to wonder how these two Justices managed to even get law degrees with such a limited view of the Constitution. I think they missed the "Life, Liberty, and Pursuit of Happiness" lecture.

They must have missed the part about the Constitution limiting the powers of the central government, NOT limiting the rights of the people.

I would think that "Life, Liberty, and the Pursuit of Happiness" would be among those rights retained by the people. I also think that these two Justices failed to consider how an innocent person could have had a "full and fair trial" yet been convicted.

I think that Justices Scalia and Thomas should be tried (and found guilty) of treason. There is no way that they should be on the US Supreme Court.

Why I Hate Republicans…

12. "Borrow and spend" is a disproportionate tax on the poor.

Why I Hate Republicans…

13. Sarah Palin.

Why I Hate Republicans…

14. Dick Cheney, someone else who should be tried for treason.

Why I Hate Republicans…


15. Fox "News."

Why I Hate Republicans…

16. Family values make good campaign slogans, until they find out about your affairs and gay lovers.

Why I Hate Republicans…

17. Has anyone told the Republicans that separation of church and state is part of the Constitution?

Why I Hate Republicans…

18. James Inhofe, one of only nine Senators who voted against the Detainee Treatment Act of 2005, which prohibits "cruel, inhuman or degrading" treatment of individuals while in custody of the U.S. Government.

Why I Hate Republicans…


19. Karl Rove.

Why I Hate Republicans…

20. Republicans were against Social Security. They were against Medicare and Medicaid. They were against Health Care Reform.

I guess when you don't have any good ideas of your own, you just oppose everything the other party suggests.

Why I Hate Republicans…

21. They're still crying about Health Care Reform. I mean come on – isn't it time they advanced to the 20$^{th}$ century? Oh, yes, I *do* know that it is now the 21$^{st}$ century.

Why I Hate Republicans…

22. I was just recently reminded of Barry Goldwater's statement that "extremism in defense of liberty is no vice!" and "moderation in pursuit of justice is no virtue."

Actually, I agree with him 100%. Now if Republicans would just do that.

Why I Hate Republicans…


23. Extraordinary Extraditions.

Why I Hate Republicans…

24. Torture.

Why I Hate Republicans…

25. An American citizen was held for two years with no charges and was not allowed to see a lawyer. How would you feel if that were you?

Why I Hate Republicans...

26. Republicans scream about how health care reform will ruin our economic freedom and destroy the Constitution.

Yet they were completely silent about warrantless wiretapping. And they still are silent about it.

Now there is a Constitutional violation with some real teeth to it, and they don't care!?

Why I Hate Republicans…

27. Speaking of "economic freedom," what is that and how will health care reform interfere with it?

How is having an insurance company deny coverage for pre-existing conditions better? How is having a lifetime cap better?

I'm just thinking that our economic freedom already has lots of things interfering with it, and the Republicans seem fine with all of those other things.

Why I Hate Republicans…

28. Did I mention that Republicans just seem to be *against* everything, without offering any good ideas of their own?

Why I Hate Republicans…

29. It seems like they want to solve *every* problem by cutting taxes.

That might solve some problems, but surely not all of them. How can a wide variety of challenges be dealt with so simplistically?

Why I Hate Republicans…

30. A quote from Richard Volaar: "They speak however innocently of individual initiative, but they actually mean that the most productive and prodigious should be given most of the available welfare, leaving those less able or fortunate than them to fight like vermin or criminals for the scraps they deign to judge us worthy of.

Most Republicans, by volume, are innocent of the actual consequences of their beliefs, but ignorance in the face of so much evidence is no longer a suitable excuse."

(He said it better than I could.)

Why I Hate Republicans…

31. The "Great Recession" of 2008.

Somehow, the warped-minded Republicans are trying to blame this on Obama.

Why I Hate Republicans…


32. Mitch McConnell.

### 33.  Blue Dog Democrats

They are the main reason why Democratic "majorities" still have trouble passing their agenda and they give Republicans an excellent means of muddying the waters.

If they rarely vote with your party, what's the point of having them in it?

Why I Hate Republicans…

34. Republicans think that tax cuts for the richest 2% are more important than nuclear arms treaties and health care for 9-1-1 responders. (As if you didn't already know who they really represent.)

Why I Hate Republicans…

35. Republicans love reading the Constitution on the floor of the House. Well, the 3/5ths of it that they approve of, anyway.

Why I Hate Republicans…

36. US Senator Joseph "Joe" McCarthy was a Republican.

Why I Hate Republicans…


37. My favorite "what ifs" of strict construction:

1) John McCain could not be President. He was not born in the US, not even in a territory.

2) You can keep and bear any arms (stinger missiles, heavy machine guns, *etc.)* but you do not have the right to *ammunition*!

Why I Hate Republicans…

38. The Constitution, the document that Republicans love to wrap around themselves, does not mention the word "capitalism" once.

Why I Hate Republicans…

39. There is no such thing as a free market in today's world. What we call "free" markets (Wall Street, commodities) are, in fact, controlled by the big banks.

If you have enough money, you can control the price of anything. The big banks have enough money.

Buy enough of a commodity and the price goes up. And who pays for this increase? The workers who buy food and other goods.

This is just another legal way to suck money from the poor and the middle class and put it in the pockets of the richest 2%.

Why I Hate Republicans…

40. And by the way, cutting taxes to the richest 2% just gives them more money to buy commodities with, which increases the prices more, which allows them to take more money from the workers. All without creating a single job.

Why I Hate Republicans…

41. Tax breaks to the richest 2% do not stimulate the economy. There is not an economist around who supports this theory.

This is only a Republican political position that favors their base – the richest 2%.

Consider this: A man has a store. We cut his taxes to 0%, but increase the taxes on his employees. If no one comes into his store to buy things, is he going to hire more people just because his taxes have been cut?

NO.

But if you put money in the hands of consumers, then more people will be able to buy the storekeeper's goods and he *will* hire more people – EVEN IF WE RAISE HIS TAXES!

Why I Hate Republicans…

42. There's a group of mostly Tea Partiers and Republicans who want to legislatively interpret the meaning of the citizenship clause of the 14th Amendment.

You know, it's the Amendment which was passed to grant citizenship to those who had been slaves, and thus were not considered to be citizens. The mechanism for doing this was simply stating that all those who had been born in the US were citizens.

The simple majesty of a simple means of dealing with the problem of granting citizenship to former slaves would be undone by simplistic simpletons who think they can legislate an interpretation of the U.S. Constitution.

If you aren't appalled by this, your patriotism should be severely questioned. Not to mention the fact that I don't think that any legal scholar thinks that it would stand up.

Why I Hate Republicans…

43. And then there's the group of Tea Partiers' (and some Republicans) who are so enthralled by the Constitution that they do not think that it should ever have been amended. Uh… except maybe for that slavery bit. Oh…and maybe that part about women voting.

Maybe I should mention that the Bill of Rights was created by Amendment….

44. And then there's yet another right-leaning group that wants us to go back to the system where state legislatures elect U.S. Senators.

The Amendment that changed the election of Senators to a vote of the people is largely attributed to the tremendous fraud that was committed in the process of electing Senators by state legislatures.

It is quite easy to buy a legislature. William Clark, in the early 1900s here in Montana, was believed to have given $100,000 in bribes to state legislators in order to get elected to the US Senate.

When this came to light, he had to resign, and the Constitution was amended shortly thereafter.

Why I Hate Republicans…

45. The Republicans talk about less federal government. They don't want Uncle Sam or any other "Big Brother" agency messing with their rights.    They are committed to the principal that the government should mind its own business and stay out of the lives and rights of others.

*Unless* …

Two consenting adults of the same sex want to be acknowledged as spouses by the courts, or …

Someone gets a permit to build an Islamic community center that is not even visible from the Ground Zero site, or …

Someone wants to stop people from protesting at funerals of fallen soldiers with inflammatory signs, or …

Someone wants to hold big business accountable for oil spills that ruin the livelihoods of tens of thousands and ruin delicate ecosystems, or …

Someone wants to keep CEOs honest by limiting the amount of money they can steal from investors.

In other words, Republicans are okay with limiting the rights of everyone else. They just don't want *their own* rights limited. And, in fact, they want the right to take advantage of everyone else.

Why I Hate Republicans…

46. Republicans complain about the federal government interfering in the rights of the people. However…

It was the federal government that stepped in and enforced the rights of the civil rights marchers.

The federal government also made sex and race discrimination illegal throughout the entire country. If that had been left to the states, I suspect that there are states where either one or both of these would still be legal.

Why I Hate Republicans…

47. "Republicans preach fear and loathing, pride and prejudice, envy and greed and every oppressive defect ever inflicted by one human being against another. And they do so with the utmost righteousness and certainty, virtually declaring themselves legally insane, or gleefully ignorant, in the process." - *Richard Volaar.*

## Why I Hate Republicans...

48. A friend recently sent me yet another right leaning email listing various stupid things attributed to Democratic politicians. None of it was true. It occurred to me that I have seen dozens of these over the past few years and not a single one had ever been factually correct. And yet I never see the same sort of emails falsely accusing Republican politicians.

It then occurred to me that someone, somewhere creates these emails, and knows they are false. And this person would certainly have to be against Democrats. What is it that they are hiding? Why do they have to create falsehoods in order to defeat their opponents? Could it be because their own agenda is so perverse?

Could this be Karl Rove's new career?

Why I Hate Republicans...

49. Revisionist History. Clinton didn't balance the budget. "W" didn't cause the deficit. 9-1-1, Afghanistan, and Iraq caused the deficit. Somehow the tax cuts and the unfunded Medicare Prescription benefit get overlooked.

Why I Hate Republicans…

50. Eric Cantor, the new Republican majority leader, who I just saw misrepresenting the words of NPR official Ron Schiller. And he did it with a smile. And the Republicans in the background laughed.

Why I Hate Republicans...


51. Voting without being well informed on the issues is the ultimate unpatriotic act. I feel that the great majority of those who vote Republican do this. They want their politics simple and concise, the truth be damned, and vote accordingly, thus making our nation worse in the process.

I have come to realize that Republicans tend to inherently mistrust everyone and everything.

Democrats tend to inherently trust everyone and everything.

The world is better off with the latter, but it is easy to see why it only takes a few of the former to prevail.